Edited by Rachel Tarwater
Book Design by Chyna Creatives and Bomi Roberson

ISBN 978-0-692-96979-3

In loving memory of Saundra Newton.
The woman who taught me to live life and walk in
the freedom of who God made me to be.
I miss and love you.

Contents

Meet Bomi

Bomi Roberson currently serves as the Women's Director at King's Park International Church. She is an avid HGTV viewer, enjoys pinning several creative ideas on Pinterest, and gets very giddy at the chance to engage in Do-It-Yourself projects. Bomi is passionate about finding beauty in the simple things. She enjoys sharing about God's love, the power of prayer, leadership, and interpersonal communication. You can often find her hanging out with her kids (most times as a Chauffer), doing a DIY project, designing invitations for special events, or working hard to figure out "what's for dinner." Bomi currently resides in Durham, North Carolina with her husband, Reggie, and three children – Nickolas, David, and Shiloh-Kemi.

Dear Sister,

Thank you for joining me on this journey to discover you are God's Plan A. It is no coincidence you are holding this book in your hands; I believe God has something special to tell you.

This study came out of a season marked by uncertainty and frustration. I felt I was a Plan B or not an option at all in many areas. I was not sure what the Lord was doing or why He permitted me to experience these gut-wrenching emotions. I couldn't see or understand God's purpose in these experiences. My confidence faded as I was passed over for job after job, project after project. As the days wore on, I began to question my worth, saying to mysef "I feel so unPreferred" But just when I started to internalize this belief, God happened! I was His Preferred all along; how could I have not seen it? LOL!

What I learned through my experience helped me trust God even when others seemed preferred over me. It set me free from the trap of unforgiveness and bitterness. I now view situations through a different lens, and I see God's hand in EVERYTHING!
This study is a journal of what God taught me, and I pray that YOU too will see how HE intricately interweaves your "so called" unPreferred experience with His purpose, power, provision and protection. YOU ARE HIS PREFERRED and have been ALL ALONG! So put your seat belts on, start the engine, and let us take a pleasant ride to *God's Plan A!*

Yours in Christ,
Bomi

How to use this book

This book is a 4-week study about how to overcome feeling unPreferred and understand how Preferred you are in God's eyes. Each week begins with a scripture to focus on and fill-in-the-blank questions to answer and discuss in a group setting. The Answer Key at the end of the book has all of the answers to the fill-in-the-blank questions but try not to look at them until after each session. The weekly devotional sections each contain five days of stories, activities, and open-ended questions to help you explore the concepts discussed in the group study in greater depth.

Study Session 1

Misfit or Ms. Fit?

Genesis 29:16-30 (HCSB)

Scripture focus Genesis 29:17 & 30
17 Leah had ordinary eyes, but Rachel was shapely and beautiful. 30 Jacob slept with Rachel also, and indeed, he loved Rachel more than Leah. And he worked for Laban another seven years.

1. God's definition of what is preferred, fit, perfect, or acceptable _____
_____; it stands the ____ __ _____ .

2. God will often use the _____ you think is imperfect for
His platform because He wants _____ __ _____. He specializes in using
what is _____ _____ _____ to reveal His wisdom.

3. Being overlooked or unPreferred, is often ____ _____ because you are
_____ _____ _____ for a _____ _____.

4. _____ to the Lord, as there may be some things that you need to
genuinely develop in your walk with Him.

Study Session 2

An unlikely king

1 Samuel 16: 1-7; 10-13 (HCSB)

Scripture Focus 1 Samuel 16:7
7 But the Lord said to Samuel, "Do not look at his appearance or his stature, because I have rejected him. Man does not see what the Lord sees, for man sees what is visible, but the Lord sees the heart."

1. God _____ ____ _____ and often uses them for His _____ _____.

2. _____ comes from God. Regardless of how circumstances, people, or systems shun, submerge, or inadvertently hide you, God can and will _____ any barrier to _____ you at the _____ _____.

3. God looks at the _____ and not _____, qualifications or looks.

4. God _____ you for what He _____ you to do.

"God will use the most unlikely person to do an unlikely thing to get an unlikely result." Christine Caine. From "Highly Unlikely" message at Life Church TV by http://live.lifechurch.tv.

Study Session 3

On the flip side

Genesis 25: 27-34 and Proverbs 18:17 (HCSB)

Scripture focus **Proverbs 18:17**
The first to state his case seems right until another comes and cross-examines him.

What we need to understand through Jacob's life:

1. As the saying goes, _hurt_ people hurt _people_. Jacob was hurt because he was not the preferred son, so he made choices that hurt his brother Esau. Perhaps people who have overlooked you have been _hurt_ in the past.

2. Jacob didn't know God for himself until much later; he only knew God from his father's experience (Genesis 27:20 and Genesis 28: 20). Those who overlook may not understand God's _plan_ because they don't see things from God's _perspective_. Often times people make choices based on their own life experience rather than God's direction.

3. Jacob's life was wrapped up in _trickery_ and _deceit_; it may have been all he knew. After all, his name was Jacob which means to undermine, to grab the heel, to supplant. The _opinion_ and _wrongdoing_ of those who overlook you often _shape_ how they _____ and _relate_ to others.

Don't take it personal
there is an expiration date

Personalize it!
Think about a situation in which you felt unPreferred. How did you feel about it before the study? Does this study give you any new insight about your situation?

Read Proverbs 2:1-6. Pray for wisdom this week.

12

Study Session 4

2 Corinthians 3:17-18

"What Say You?"

Scripture Focus A scriptural promise or your favorite verse.

1. _____ _____.

Take Him at His word. You are and have always been His plan A. He is the best CEO of your life and knows what is best. Take Him at His word and believe Him.

2. ___ _____.

We all have preferences. We exercise the right to choose our preference when we shop, when we eat, when we make friends and more. Those who have overlooked you may not even know they have done so, so we must be kind and patient.

3. _____ _____.

There are many instances in the Bible where the people who have been overlooked were finally recognized while they were doing what they do on a regular basis. David, Joseph, and Gideon are a few examples.

4. Find your _____/ _____.

 Please watch this video (link below) by Micheal Jr. Begin at 22:33 minute mark.

http://gatewaypeople.com/sermons/264491

Our punchline is when we respond differently from what others expect. It is when we respond in a Godly manner, seeking to give love rather than always looking to receive it.

Weekly Devo 1

Day 1 Fruitful

Read Genesis 29: 31.

Have you ever been in a conversation with someone who says so little but means so much? I have, and what is said is rarely forgotten. I believe this is the case with today's devotional verse. Go ahead and read it again, only this time a bit slower so you can capture more of what is happening in this verse.

1. What do you see?
Hint: pay close attention to the words unloved/ not loved; noticed/ saw; and womb.

Biblical scholars believe God compensated Leah by opening her womb because Jacob did not love her. In those days it was a sign of God's favor to have children, especially sons. So even though Leah was not seen by her husband, GOD TOOK NOTICE OF HER and made her FRUITFUL!

2. What do you think this says about what God thinks of you?

Dear loved one, even though you find yourself in a situation where you are not preferred, overlooked, unappreciated, or simply told that you are plan B, you need to know:

1) GOD SEES YOU, and you are never forgotten. Take a moment and let it resonate. Say to yourself (7 times) I AM NOT FORGOTTEN, GOD SEES ME!

2) GOD WILL MAKE YOU FRUITFUL. Leah was fruitful even though she was considered Jacob's Plan B (in fact, not his plan at all). Take a moment to reflect and think of a situation (or situations) in which you are a plan B or not a plan. Ask God to open your eyes to how He has made you fruitful. You may be surprised as you start to notice God's favor and blessing in your life.

What do you think about this? Please write your thoughts and remember you are God's Preferred, God's plan A. YOU ARE FRUITFUL and NOT FORGOTTEN.

Day 2 Focused

Genesis 29: 32-34

Looking back, I am almost embarrassed to share this story. However, it is so applicable to today's devotional, so here I go into the land of vulnerability. FEEL FREE to laugh. No, Seriously 😀
In Nigeria, where I grew up, it was very common for students to go to boarding school for what is equivalent to Middle and High school in America. I was in Junior Secondary School II, which is the 7th grade. We had just returned from summer break, and I was still riding on the excitement of "supposedly" being mature and older. I was mature to a certain extent with the exception of one area - BOYS! I wasn't crazy about them; I just thought one in particular was really cute. I dressed up every day with my uniform ironed and my braided hair neatly brushed hoping he would notice me. One day I couldn't take it any longer and I decided to put some makeup on, hoping to finally get his attention. When I got to class, my friends looked at me with surprise, and the boy hardly spoke to me. I thought to myself, "Finally he finds me so attractive that he is speechless and my friends are stunned by my beauty." I later learned my perception was far from the truth. The reality was that I - in my inexperience - had used the wrong powder all over my face, making it a brick red color. My friends thought I looked crazy, and my crush has asked what was wrong with me! I wanted to sink into the ground when I heard about these reactions. Long story short...he was attracted to another friend the whole time. He even dated her for a stint.
I tried to get this boy's attention by dressing up and attempting to put on makeup. Similarly, Leah thought doing something would win her husband's attention.

1.What did Leah think would gain her husband's love?

2. How many sons did Leah have in these two verses?

3. Match the name to its meaning.

Simeon   seen my affliction

Levi   attached to

Reuben   has heard

4. Do you think the fact that Leah gave her husband sons will win his love? Why or Why not?

As you recall from yesterday, having sons was not only a sign of strength for the father but also a sign of God's favor. Because of this, Leah expected to find approval and acceptance by giving Jacob sons. Unfortunately, that was not the case. Like Leah, we too can get caught up in doing XYZ to gain approval or to feel preferred. Perhaps you have been turned down for a promotion, so you begin to take professional classes you don't enjoy to boost your credentials in hopes it will land you the next promotion.Or maybe you are single and have watched many of your friends get married, so you start thinking up different ideas to make yourself more "marketable" to men. I could go on and on. But these kinds of attempts will do much more harm than good. Why? Because they are NOT FOCUSED ON GOD. They are man-made attempts to fix something only God can repair.

5. Read Genesis 29:35. What happened to Leah?

6. What was the name of her fourth son? What does his name mean?

By the time her fourth son, Judah, was born, Leah realized that her hope comes from God alone. Not from Jacob. Not from bearing children. HER HOPE CAME FROM GOD. With this realization, she shifted her focus to Him. In the same way, we need to trust God with our desire to be preferred and let Him direct our next steps. Focus on Him and let him be the comfort you seek, the approval you want, the validation you long for. When our focus is on Him, we experience a freedom that leaves no room for disappointment.

TAKE IT A STEP FURTHER

Ask God to show you any behaviors, decisions, or habits you have created to compensate for feeling un-preferred or overlooked. Ask God to forgive you for taking matters into your hands through these habits and ask Him to help you shift your FOCUS to HIM.

Day 3 Faith-full

If you ever want the Bible to become very real to you, ask God. What happens next is amazing! When I was younger I prayed to the Lord to make His word alive in a fresh and revelatory way. I wanted to see the connections between what happened in Biblical times and the experiences people have in the present day. Well, God heard my prayer. I suddenly found myself asking unusual questions about what I read in the Bible, and these questions pushed me to learn more. One of these ridiculous questions came up when I read about King Solomon. I asked my husband, "How come the Bible doesn't talk about Solomon having an sexually transmitted infection or disease if he had so many wives and concubines?" Well, my husband replied, "Perhaps they brought him virgins." My response, "Good for Solomon, but incredibly unfair to every qualified bachelor who now loses every chance of getting a wife to the King." If you are laughing, I was too. Although crazy, these questions caused me to dive deeper into His word. A similar situation occurred in our text regarding Leah being un-preferred. Let's read it together.

Genesis 29: 31-35 (MSG).

31-32 When God realized that Leah was unloved, he opened her womb. But Rachel was barren. Leah became pregnant and had a son. She named him Reuben (Look-It's-a-Boy!). "This is a sign," she said, "that God has seen my misery; and a sign that now my husband will love me." 33-35 She became pregnant again and had another son. "God heard," she said, "that I was unloved and so he gave me this son also." She named this one Simeon (God-Heard). She became pregnant yet again—another son. She said, "Now maybe my husband will connect with me—I've given him three sons!" That's why she named him Levi (Connect). She became pregnant a final time and had a fourth son. She said, "This time I'll praise God." So she named him Judah (Praise-God). Then she stopped having children.

1. Yesterday, we read about Leah shifting her focus from Jacob to God. How do we know this happened?

2. What does the name "Judah" mean?

3. What happened between Levi and Judah?

Although the Bible doesn't explain or even tell us the time frame between the boys, we know it was at least nine months. So what happened to Leah's heart in those nine months? Why and how did Leah shift her focus from gaining Jacob's approval to only PRAISING GOD?

The answer, I believe, is found in the story of Abraham, who the Bible considers the father of faith. Read Romans 4:18-25 (ESV).

4. Abraham grew in his unwavering faith as he did what? (see verse 20)

Giving glory to God communicated his total trust in God's ability to do something in a circumstance that was considered unchangeable. It also took his attention off of the unfulfilled promise and on God.

Lamentation 3:25-27 (MSG) says:

> *God proves to be good to*
> *the man who passionately waits,*
> *to the woman who diligently seeks.*
> *It's a good thing to quietly hope,*
> *quietly hope for help from God.*
> *It's a good thing when you're young*
> *to stick it out through the hard times.*

5. What does it mean to "quietly hope"?

6. What ultimately happens when we quietly hope for help from God?

Somewhere between Levi and Judah, Leah realized that her hope came only from God. God is good to those who hope in him. Those who trust in the Lord will not be forsaken. Those who look to God to satisfy their deepest needs and desires will never be ashamed. Those who wait on God and give glory to Him will GROW IN FAITH. And their FAITH will be counted as RIGHTEOUSNESS (right standing with God). How about that?! Leah uncovered a secret. She discovered that when she set her eyes on God and PRAISED HIM, her attitude changed, her focus on God grew stronger, and her focus on Jacob lessenend. This proved true even though her circumstances stayed the same.

Today, as you quietly wait on God to be known as the preferred one, the PLAN A, would you give God glory in spite of your circumstance? Would you give Him a chance to prove His love to you? Praise HIM as if you are already preferred and see your focus shift toward God. Watch as He makes you Faith-FULL regarding His promise to you.

Day 4 Foresight

A story is never a good one without a climactic end, and God always writes a fantastic story! Just when you think your decision to believe God is only for your well being or the realization of His promise, God reveals a much bigger plan. His plan. His plan blesses generations; God blesses you so others can experience His glory as well. It is not just about you.

From this week's devotional we learned how God blessed Leah and made her fruitful in spite of her despair. We also watched how she turned her heart toward God when she felt unloved by Jacob. Leah ultimately believed GOD and gave Him Glory even when things did not appear to be improving in her life. It was in this decision that she birthed Judah, and here comes the WOW factor...drum roll, please... JESUS HAPPENED!

Did you know that Jesus, our Lord, and Savior, came from the lineage of Judah? What a powerful testimony! Judah was the one borne out of a heart that looked to God. Not only did God bless Leah with peace of mind, He also gave her a son whose loins would carry the Son of God. What a privilege! The Savior of the world came from a woman who was unloved, unwanted, un-preferred, a plan B!

1. What do you think about this right now?

God is a good Father; He will give you a double share of honor for your shame and reproach (Isaiah 61:7). In the meantime trust Him, believe Him and know that something amazing will come from you. When you take your focus off being unpreferred and place it on God, the results will go beyond your wildest dreams.

You are loved and preferred by God, and He is birthing something great in you!

Day 5 Forward Thinking

Have you enjoyed this week's study? I hope it has opened your eyes to see how much God thinks of you despite what you initially thought or what others have said. Today, I don't have any scriptures or stories to share, just a word of encouragement.

God is madly in love with you and notices every challenge you are facing. So when you find yourself in a context where another person is chosen or preferred over you, say this quick prayer:

"Father, I know You love me. I choose to believe I am Your Preferred even when my circumstances don't make me feel like it. I praise You, and I thank You for having the whole picture in Your hands."

Take a few moments to review what you have learned throughout this week's study by answering the questions below.

1. What stood out to you?

2. What spoke to your situation the most?

3. How did it help you?

4. How do you intend to see things God's way going forward?

Ponder these questions and let God speak to you. I have no doubt your time of contemplation will prepare you for next week's focus - God's Sovereignty. You are loved. YOU ARE PREFERRED!

Weekly Devo 2

Day 1 Smart & Sovereign

1 Samuel 16:1-3
Many adjectives describe the character of God, and the two I have come to appreciate of late are SMART and SOVEREIGN.

1. Go to the dictionary, how does it define:
    1. SMART as an adjetive:

    2. SOVEREIGN as an adjective:

2. What did God ask Samuel to do?

3. How did Samuel respond?

4. Has God asked you to do something at an awkward or inconvenient time? What was it?

5. How did you respond?

God asked Samuel to anoint (rub oil conferring a divine appointment) someone else king while Saul was still on the throne. Samuel knew that if Saul ever found out about this, his own life would be in danger. You see, anointing someone in leadership while the current leader is still in place could communicate a takeover. In other words, the ruler is asked (or forced) to give up their throne. In a panic, Samuel reminded God of this dilemma, and God immediately provided him with a solution. Although it seems this text may be a bit off the subject, it is not. It will make more sense through tomorrow's devotional. This is more of a side lesson, a pit stop if you will, to say, there are times when God may ask us to do something at the most inopportune moments, and if we are not careful, we can analyze our way out of His leading, believing His directive could be a bad idea especially when we feel unpreferred. Are you in a moment like this? Be encouraged! Sometimes God will defy logic to establish His Sovereignty. You serve a SMART God. His solutions will never compromise your integrity or be contrary to His word. So when you find yourself in an unusual position based on what the Lord has spoken to you, always ask God for wisdom on how to carry out His plan. It's important to point out that David's quiet anointing was part of God's plan all along. God is not limited by culture, economy, or standards. In fact, He often does things at seemingly inconvenient or incorrect times to reveal His power and glory so that His SOVEREIGNTY is amplified.

6. Have you ever been in a situation where you were unsure how to show honor and maintain your integrity?
Have you said to yourself, "This is the worst time for this to happen!"?

7. If so, in light of what you have just read, what do you think now?

Remember that even in those moments when you are UNPREFERRED, God has an award-winning solution and is waiting for you to ask Him for it. He is SMART and SOVEREIGN, always working out His plan A in the background.

Day 2 Power of a SEED
1 Samuel 16:7

A few years ago I went to a plant store to purchase some tree stakes for our evergreens. The store needed to get rid of their leftover stock, so they were giving it away for free. I took the bag with gratitude but was warned by the store attendant that most of the bulbs were dried out and would likely not yield any flowers.

Well, I got home, stashed the brown bag in a cabinet and forgot about it. A year later we were cleaning out the cabinet and found the bag. Even though we were convinced the seeds had died nine times over and needed to be trashed, we decided to give them a shot.

Well... The most beautiful lilies ended up blooming. More than that, they continued to multiply. We uprooted them and moved them to another location, and even there they continued to thrive and reproduce in following spring and summer. I thought the seeds were dead. I was convinced the bulbs had no life. How wrong I was! Those seeds and bulbs carried so much beauty inside; they just needed to be planted and nurtured to reach their potential.

Although small, dry, and unusual in appearance, a seed carries the genetic material to become a beautiful flower or a big tree. A seed carries amazing potential even when it doesn't look like it.

When God looks at us, He sees the whole package - matured or not, seed or tree. That was what He was communicating to Samuel when Samuel expressed concern about anointing David for leadership while Saul was still King. You see, God is SMART and SOVERGEIGN. God appreciates and values us, even in seed (undeveloped) form.

1.What did God tell Samuel in Verse 7?

2. Read I Samuel 16: 5-7. Do you think Samuel would have anointed the wrong person if God did not intervene? Why?

God is never impressed with how we look or what we do. Rather, our faith and the contents of our hearts is what moves Him. Often, we dismiss opportunities because we fail to look beyond the surface and see what God sees. Samuel could have anointed the wrong son to be King had God not spoken to him. God sees the potential and power of a seed and wants you to see it as well.

3. What about you? Have you disregarded an ordinary opportunity only to learn later on it was what you needed if you only took the time to see it through God's eyes and nurture it with God's love?

4. Let us look at this from another perspective. Is there an ability, trait, you have dismissed because you were told it can work against you ? For instance, not trying out for a sport because you think you are too tall or too short? Not applying for a position because you don't fit some of the qualifying criteria? Shunning an opportunity because you do not feel equipped?

5. What do you sense the Holy Spirit is saying to you about this at this moment?

Just because something looks unusual or unassuming doesn't mean it lacks potential. Ask God to give you His vision so you can see, from His perspective, the potential of the seed He placed in you.
You are PREFERRED!

Day 3 You Called Me What?!

1 Samuel 16:11 (MSG)
Then he asked Jesse, "Is this it? Are there no more sons?" "Well, yes, there's the runt. But he's out tending the sheep." Samuel ordered Jesse, " Go get him. We're not moving from his spot until he's here."

1.Could I walk alongside you on memory lane for a few minutes? Think back to when you were growing up, what nickname(s) did you have?

2. Do you remember why or how you got the name(s)? Please share.

3. Were these names connected to your personality or a trait you have?

4. Did you like the nickname or would you have preferred not to be called such a name?

5. Read the scripture printed at the top of this page. What was David called?

6. Take out your dictionary. How does it define this nickname?

Two things to note in this text...was David included when Jesse's sons appeared before Samuel?

What happened when Samuel realized none of the sons presented to him was God's choice?

David was called the "RUNT." Scholars believe David was an illegitimate child and treated like an outcast as a result. But the Bible says when Samuel saw David, he thought he was healthy, bright-eyed, and good looking. How is it possible that Jesse called David a Runt and yet Samuel saw something different?

My nickname growing up was Shubby Pepeye. Pepeye means duck in Yoruba (Yoruba is my native Nigerian language) and Shubby was a short form of my partial full name Subomi. My friends gave me this name because they said I ran like a duck. I didn't particularly like the name but accepted it, as it quickly became what I was known by among my peers. Over time, the name made me self-conscious, especially when I ran, affecting my participation in club races. I was a good sprinter but refused to compete because I was concerned people would ridicule me while cheering the name 'Shubby Pepeye.' Yes, it was supposed to be a term of endearment, but it affected my self-confidence instead.

My real name, however, is Olasubomi, Bomi for short, and it means "the Glory of God surrounds me". My grandfather gave me my name and when he did, he did not base it off of a trait, personality, looks, or the way I ran; he gave me my name because that was his impression from God. The meaning of my name had nothing to do with ducks; it had everything to do with God. When I began to appreciate the true meaning of my name, it changed my outlook. Don't get me wrong, nicknames are cool, but not when it begins to change who God says you are. I don't know if I still run like a duck. I couldn't tell because my focus shifted to what God calls me. In other words, I only respond to the names given to me that align with what God calls me.

Going back to the question a few paragraphs ago, how is it possible that Jesse called David a Runt while Samuel saw something different? It is because Samuel was seeing David from God's perspective. And once David heard this, he accepted the truth of how God sees him as his reality. He was satisfied with God defining him. How do we know this? Psalm 139: 13-16.

Going back to the first few questions in today's devotional, were any of your nicknames negative ones? Have you accepted them as true? Are they in alignment with what God calls you? Take some time today in prayer and ask God to remind
you of what HE calls you. Let His words and His face shine on you and outshine what others have called you. Why? The answer is in Isaiah 62:12.
You are PREFERRED!

Day 4 The Dark Room Part I

1 Samuel 16:13-18

In the same moment David was anointed, the Spirit of God left Saul, and he was in need of a minstrel. David was the man for the job. Why? Because someone in the King's court had engaged with David in his moments of obscurity and had nothing but great things to say about him. In other words, David was promoted for being himself and doing what he was called to do when no one seemed to notice. At the God-appointed time, someone remembered his skill and nominated him to serve as a minstrel for the King. In David's un-preferred, obscure, "no one knows me" moments, something was happening. I have provided a link to a message by Christine Cain. The title is called "The Dark Room". Please take some time today to listen to it. Be encouraged and blessed by it! Although you may feel un-preferred, do not despair, you may be in your Dark Room awaiting the final reveal!

https://youtu.be/ipj_XWx8wiE
(You can also visit youtube.com and type in Christine Caine Dark Room)

Day 5 The Dark Room Part II

1 Samuel 16:18-23

Did you get a chance to watch the message from Christine Caine yesterday? How did that make you feel? Please send me a note; I am curious to hear your thoughts. I appreciate how she encouraged us not to take those quiet moments for granted, as they serve as the foundation of what God does in our lives when we do come to a place of being preferred. It allows us to build our hope in God and not on man. Our text today highlights how David's gift in music soothed King Saul so much so that he asked for David to stay with him. David's appearance before Saul, also divinely orchestrated, would not have been possible had David not
honed his musical skill during the times of obscurity, in the moments when he was not preferred.
Read these two scriptures and let the Holy Spirit speak to you about sharpening your gifts, especially in seasons when you feel un-preferred or looked over. Please feel free to share your thoughts below.

Proverbs 22:29

Proverbs 18:16

Weekly 3 Devo

Day 1 Ask God

1 Samuel 16:13-18

Read Proverbs 2: 4-6 (AMP).

1. Write this scripture in your words.

2. How does the dictionary define 'omniscient'?

3. Take the definition of omniscient and replace it with the word 'knowledge' in verse 5 in the Amplified Bible (AMP) How do you see this scripture now, and what is it saying to you?

4. How do you feel knowing that God is Omniscient and is aware of ALL things?

5. Now that you know God is aware of ALL things, have you ever asked Him for insight into situations concerning being overlooked? Please give a reason for your answer.

There is a promise from God in Jeremiah 33:3. Please read and write what this scripture says to you in your words.

6. Do you believe this promise?

Many Christians know they can go to God in prayer and through His word regarding anything in their lives but do not. Some fear what the Lord would say, as it may be contrary to what they want to do in their hearts. Others may lack confidence that they will hear from God, so they never bother to try. Either position prevents us from gaining the insight we need to walk in love and freedom. It keeps us from knowing the truth.

God has promised a few things in Jeremiah 33:3. These particular promises require us to do something first.:
1) Call unto ME Your part
    I will answer you God's part
2) Call unto ME Your part
    I will show you great and mighty things you do not know God's Part

When you call out to God, He will answer you and then show you things you never knew. It is a promise.
There usually is another side to the story - the narrative of the one who does not prefer us. Knowing the perspective of the one who does not prefer you or overlooked you not only provides understanding, it gives us more information to help us manage our response to being unpreferred. You may be thinking, "What are the chances of learning about the other side of the story, especially if the situation was an extreme one?" The chances are slim, but we have an asset - our Sovereign and Omniscient God. Many do not realize we have this asset, and when they do, they rarely take advantage of believing God's promise to answer us when we call and to show us things we do not know. So in the context of our study of being unPreferred, it is pertinent that we ask God to give insight to the other side of the story of why we feel we are being overlooked, un-preferred or set as the plan B. You will be amazed by what God shows or chooses not to show you. Either way, your willingness to understand and the knowledge you gain will transform your view of the whole situation. Just ask God.

Day 2 Judging Intentions

Read Proverbs 2:1-6 (MSG) version.

Our weekly family schedule is quite full. I don't get home from work until about 5:30 pm and by the time dinner, homework, playtime, bath time and bedtime are over it is about 9:30 pm. And this is even before I get to doing anything for myself On a particular day, I scheduled to meet up with a friend (as every woman needs). I made sure dinner was ready and dashed out the door.

I returned from an excellent time hanging out only to find the kids playing. No one had taken baths, and they were not in bed. I was sure my husband would have at least started the process with hopes of easing the evening load, but that wasn't the case. NOW I had to get them ready for a bath, give them a bath, get them dressed and then get them in bed. It was as if I never left the house and my evening got prolonged. Aaah, I felt discouraged!

After the boys had gone to bed, I had a little talk with my husband and shared my frustrations with him. I expected the boys to at least have their bath by the time I returned, so they remained on the evening schedule as it had always been. Of course, my husband was apologetic and proceeded to explain that he lost track of time as he had devoted the evening to having un-interrupted playtime with them. After hearing his reasoning, I felt bad. Why? Well, when I came home and realized the kids were not even ready for a bath I had deduced that my husband wanted me to do ALL the work whether I was home or not. This thought spiraled into accusations and got me fired up. I judged my husband's actions - not giving the boys a bath, without seeking to hear what his intentions were - having an uninterrupted time of play. If I had controlled my thoughts and believed the best as Philippians 4:8 says to do, I would not have gotten so upset that evening and would have been in a better mind to ask what was happening. And after hearing my husband's intentions, I would have allowed the boys to play a little longer that evening. Instead, I did not seek insight and judged my husband's actions instead of his heart.

Our text encourages us to find insight like a prospector panning for gold or as if we are on a quest that our lives depend on it. Seeking insight means we look beyond the surface and work to understand intentions. It allows us to believe the best and gain more understanding about a matter so we can respond in Love.

Have you ever been accused of doing something you had no idea you did? What was it?

How did it make you feel?

What did you do or say afterwards?

Have you ever confronted someone on something they did only to learn their intentions were for your benefit? What was it?

How did it make you feel?

What did you do or say afterward?

How similar or different are your responses from #3 and #6?

Do they align with what Phillipians 4:8 says?

As you begin to pray for insight about the situations in which you feel over-looked on unpreferred, work to judge intentions rather than actions because intentions reveal what's in a person's heart. And even if the intentions are to do you harm, take it a step further: love and forgive. It will be an honorable way to respond because you are God's child - ALREADY PREFERRED!

Day 3 Emotional Inventory Part 1

Read Psalm 51:6 (AMP) and Psalm 62:5

In the context of this study, emotional inventory is defined as the feelings and thoughts you have for a particular situation. Using this definition, take a moment and make an emotional inventory of something that consistently bothers you about being unpreferred. List them below:

1. _____

2. _____

3. _____

4. _____

5. _____

Which items on your list fall under the following emotional categories:

1. Fear:

2. Unbelief:

3. Lack of Confidence:

4. Disappointment:

5. Discouragement:

6. Insecurity:

7. Feel free to add your category

Now, I want you to spend time identifying what God says about these categories. Do a google search and type in " biblical scriptures on _____ ". You fill in the blank with any of the categories.

Here is a personal example:

Emotional Inventory:
I wonder if I would ever be good enough for that opportunity.
The category:
Lack of Confidence and Fear.
What the scriptures say about this:
2 Peter 1:3.
God has given me everything I need for life and godliness, and this includes being equipped to do what He calls me to do.
Remember: YOU ARE PREFERRED

Day 4 Emotional Inventory Part II

Have you been thinking of yesterday's list? We are going to take it a step further today.

Spend time in worship to God. Put on your favorite worship song and focus your attention on Him. I want you to tell the Lord about your emotional inventory. Talk to Him like you would a close friend.

Then ask Him to change your thinking and feelings so that they are in alignment with what His Word (the scripture you found) says about you.

Enjoy your time with God. Hope to hear what God shows or speaks to you during this time.

Here is some space for anything you need to journal.

Day 5 Emotional Inventory Part III

Psalm 51:6

One of the things I cannot stand is a clogged up drain in a bathtub. Not only do you have to clean the bathtub because of the ring it leaves behind, but it is also just plain yucky! The experience gives me such an appreciation for Drano! I love the way it works; you pour it into the drain, it does its thing by eating up all the gunk, and viola! Water goes down the drain with absolutely no holdup.

The exercise we did for the past couple of days was our Drano. The purpose was to expose any emotional gunk in our hearts and get it all out so that we can allow the word of God in to do its work in us.

Psalm 51:6 says God desires truth in our inner being. He wants us to come to him and be honest about how we feel about things; in other words, get the emotional gunk out because confession or verbally expressing how we sincerely feel to God allows for healing in our soul. It also puts us in a place of surrender before Him. It allows Him to reveal His wisdom (His solution to our concerns) in our heart - God pours in His life and truth that allows us to function as the PREFERRED daughters that we are in spite of what others have said or our circumstances.

SO, for today's devotional…I want you to praise God and walk in the freedom that you are HIS PREFERRED

Answer Key

Answer Key

Week 1
1) Never Changes; test of time
2) Characteristic/feature; all of the glory;
   ordinary or unfavorable; unpopular
3) God's protection; THE most FIT; specific purpose
4) Be open

Week 2
1) Prefers the unwanted; divine purpose
2) Promotion; move anything; elevate; appointed time
3) Looks at the heart; credentials
4) Equips you; calls you

Week 3
1) Hurt; people; overlooked; overlook;
2) God's plan; God's perspective
3) Trickery;deceit; upbringing; environment;
   often shape; think; relate

Week 4
1) Believe God
2) Be compassionate
3) Carry on
4) Purpose/ Punchline

64940851R00029

Made in the USA
Middletown, DE
20 February 2018